AF225745

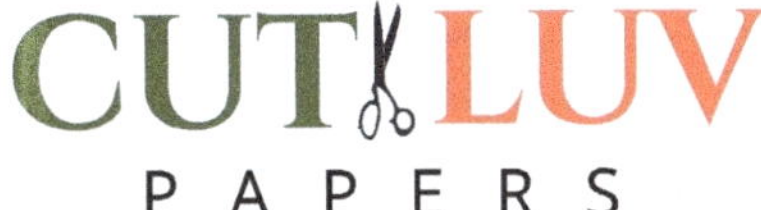

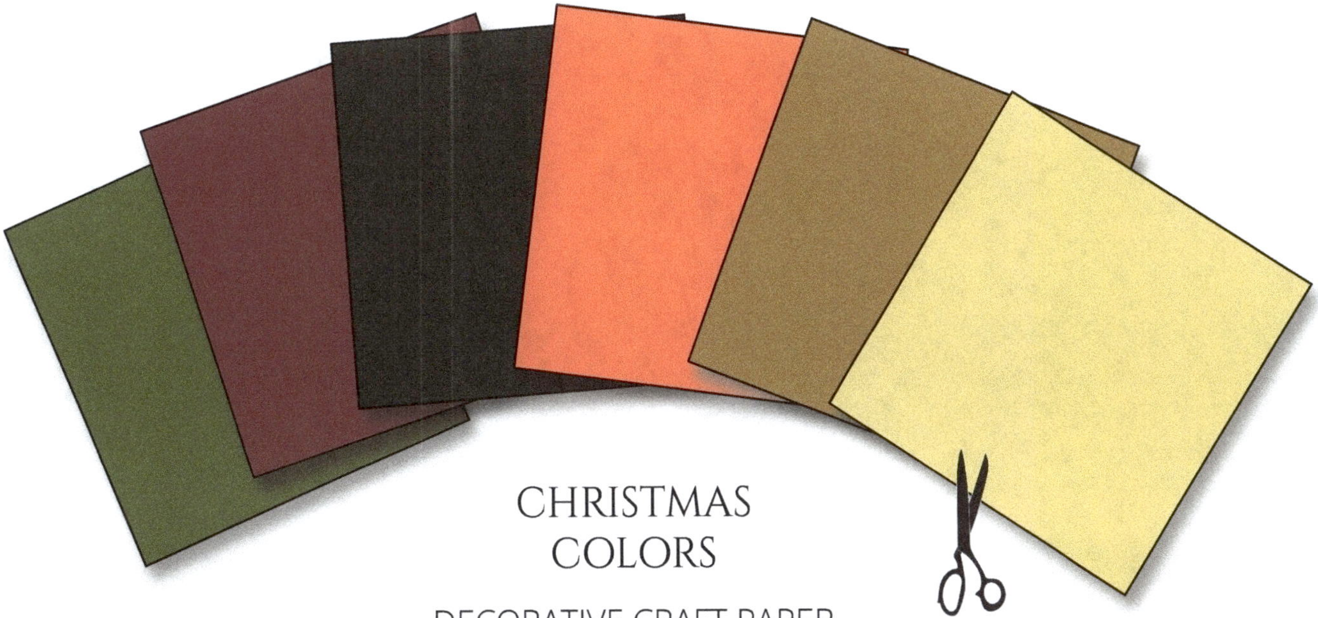

CHRISTMAS COLORS

DECORATIVE CRAFT PAPER
8 x 8 | 12 SHEETS 2 OF EACH
6 COLORS

REMOVE WITH SCISSORS